GREAT PETS

Cats

Joyce Hart

 **Marshall Cavendish**
Benchmark
New York

With thanks to Scott R. Miner, DVM,
for his expert review of the manuscript.

Marshall Cavendish Benchmark
99 White Plains Road
Tarrytown, New York 10591-9001
www.marshallcavendish.us

Library of Congress Cataloging-in-Publication Data

Hart, Joyce, date
Cats / by Joyce Hart.
p. cm. — (Great pets)
Summary: "Describes the characteristics and behavior of pet cats, also
discussing the physical appearance and place in the history of pet
cats"—Provided by publisher.
ISBN 978-0-7614-2710-0
1. Cats—Juvenile literature. I. Title.
SF445.7.H375 2008
636.8—dc22
2007016462

Photo research by Candlepants, Inc.
Front cover credit: M. Rutz/Zefa/Corbis
The photographs in this book are used by permission and through the courtesy of: *Marshall Cavendish Image Library:* 1,
40. *Peter Arnold Inc.:* Gerard Lacz, 4; PHONE Labat Jean-Michel, 9; BIOS Klein & Hubert, 14, 20, 42 (left), back cover;
BIOS Alcalay Jean-Jacques, 18; Reinhard, H., 21; Wegner, P., 23; OS Klein & Hubert, 24; BIOS Klein & Hubert, 26; BIOS
Gunther Michel, 32; PHONE Labat J.M. / F. Rouquette, 38; PHONE Labat Jean-Michel, 43. *Art Resource, NY:* HIP, 6.
Animals Animals: Donald Specker, 7; Sydney Thomson, 12; Scott W. Smith, 37. *Corbis:* Fine Art Photographic Library, 8;
Jose Luis Pelaez, Inc., 10; Jim Craigmyle, 17. *Photo Researchers Inc.:* Alan Carey, 13, 39. *Super Stock:* Zarember Preferred,
16; Age fotostock, 22, 27, 35, 42 (right); Fogstock LLC, 30. *Minden Pictures:* Mitsuaki Iwago, 25. *AP Images:* Chitose
Suzuki, 28; Corpus Christi Caller Times, John Kennedy, 29; Ben Margot, 41.

Editor: Karen Ang
Publisher: Michelle Bisson
Art Director: Anahid Hamparian
Series Designer: Elynn Cohen

Printed in Malaysia
6 5 4 3 2

Contents

1

Feline Friends

Cats of all kinds are present in the legends, religion, mythology, and history of many different cultures. Cave paintings created by early humans display different types of wild cats that are now extinct, or no longer around. Many of these great beasts saw humans as food, but were hunted by humans in return.

Cats similar to the ones kept as pets today started showing up in artwork thousands of years ago. For example, the ancient Egyptians believed cats were the sacred, or special, animal of a goddess named Bast. They believed that Bast often appeared as a cat, so many ancient Egyptians respected and honored cats and kittens. However, other cultures feared cats or thought that they brought illnesses and bad luck.

Today, with millions kept as pets in homes around the world, cats have become important members of many families.

Some cat breeds, such as the Persian, have been around for many centuries.

Cats as Pets

No one knows for sure when or how cats became very popular household pets. It is possible that people noticed how cats hunted mice and rats, so they set food and milk out to keep the cats near their homes. This helped to prevent too many of these rodents from coming into homes and eating people's food or spreading sickness. Many people today still keep barn cats on their farms. These cats are not usually house pets, but live around barns and other structures where there are large populations of mice and rats for the cats to hunt.

Hunting skills may have been the first reason why humans started caring for cats, but people soon realized that having a cat as a pet could be a wonderful experience. Cats that were kept as pets were often cute and cuddly companions.

These bronze figures were made by ancient Egyptians who honored the goddess Bast.

A barn cat takes a break from hunting mice to nap in the afternoon sunshine.

The reasons cats make good pets are different for each person. Some people like cats because cats can be very independent. This means that they do not need to be closely watched all the time. Many cats keep themselves entertained if you give them a few toys. They can take outdoor walks on their own. Cats also do not need much training, and you do not have to bathe them very often.

As shown in this painting by George Sheridan Knowles,
kittens have long been a popular addition to many families.

A kitten can be a perfect playmate.

Other people like cats because they can be very affectionate, or loving. Many cats love to follow their humans around the house, crawling into laps or rubbing against legs and hands in search of attention.

Whatever their reasons may be, many people agree that cats make perfect pets.

2

Is a Cat Right for You?

Bringing a pet into your home is an exciting event. However, you must remember that it is also a big responsibility. Before getting any kind of pet, you must make sure that you are ready for it. It might help to ask yourself and your family some of the following questions.

Do I Have Space for a Cat?

Most cats do not get very big, so they do not need a lot of space. This is one reason why many people who live in apartments or small houses have cats. Still, you must make sure you have enough space for it to move around and for things such as its food dishes, its toys, its bed or sleeping area, and its **litter box**.

There are more than 70 million cats living as pets in homes across the United States.

Chasing leaves is a fun game for this outdoor cat.

Some people like to let their cats live outdoors or at least spend some time outdoors. If that is the case, then you must be sure you live in an area that is safe for your outdoor cat. Are there a lot of dangers that could hurt the cat, such as busy traffic, wild animals, or **stray** cats and dogs? Does the cat have somewhere to stay if it is cold or wet outside or if it needs to hide from danger?

If you have other pets, such as birds, hamsters, or dogs, do you have enough space for a cat? Many families have a variety of pets that get along

This guinea pig and kitten are friends, but not all household pets will get along. Always be careful when introducing your new cat to other animals.

You can keep your cat or kitten busy with fun toys or other objects that they can safely play with.

really well. But not every cat and dog will get along. In the wild, cats hunt small animals like birds and rodents. If you have a pet bird, a hamster, or a guinea pig, you must be sure that your new cat cannot hurt it. Some dogs enjoy the company of cats, while others do not. Sometimes cats and dogs living together in one home need their own spaces. This may prevent them from fighting or bothering each other. You should consider these things before adding another animal to your household.

ALLERGIES

Allergies are your body's reaction to things you touch, eat, or breathe in. For example, in the springtime you may sneeze a lot or get itchy eyes because of all the pollen (tiny particles) from the flowers and trees that are blooming. This is an allergic reaction to the pollen in the air. Some people are allergic to certain foods. The foods may cause their skin to itch or swell and the foods may even cause breathing problems.

People can also be allergic to certain animals. A lot of people are allergic to cats. A simple allergic reaction to cats may include sneezing, watery eyes, or itchy bumps on the skin. In other cases, however, a person who is allergic to cats can have serious problems breathing and may need to go to a hospital for treatment.

Before you decide to get a cat, you need to know if you are allergic to it. The best and safest way to do this is to ask your doctor. He or she can discuss allergies with you and perhaps run some tests to see if you are allergic to cats. Do not try to test your allergies by petting a cat and seeing if you react. This can be dangerous if you have serious allergies!

Do I Have Time for a Cat?

Most cats are independent. Unlike dogs, they do not need to be put on a leash and walked outside several times a day. Also, indoor cats are trained to go to the bathroom in a litter box. Cats can provide their own fun and exercise by running or climbing around your home, or playing with toys you provide.

Kittens love spending time with their human friends.

But even if they are independent, many cats still want to spend time with their humans. They may demand attention by jumping into your lap, winding themselves around your legs as you walk, or by making a lot of noise. You must be sure you can spend some part of your day and evening playing with and petting your feline friend.

You will also need to make time to take care of your cat's basic needs. This includes feeding and cleaning up after your pet. Though you do not have to bathe your cat very often, you still need to groom it. This means brushing its fur—especially if it is long—and making sure its claws are short.

Bringing your cat to the vet for regular check ups and whenever it is sick help to keep it healthy.

You must also take time to bring your cat to the **veterinarian** (or vet for short) for regular check ups or whenever it is sick.

Carefully thinking about all of these things will help you decide if a cat is the right pet for you.

3

Choosing a Cat

Once you have decided to get a cat, there are still many more decisions you will have to make before bringing it home. Careful research can help make these decisions easier.

Cat or Kitten?

When choosing a pet cat, you should think about how old it is. Do you want a baby cat, or kitten, or do you want an older cat? Kittens are tiny and cute, but they also have a lot of energy. Kittens are more likely to run and climb around a lot. They will also need a lot more attention while they are growing. Adult cats can have a lot of energy, too, but older cats are usually a little calmer. When choosing a cat, some people say that age does not matter, as long as the cat's personality is sweet and fun.

Many families enjoy having more than one cat in their homes.

Different cat breeds can have different body features. Unlike many other breeds, this Japanese bobtail cat has a short—or bobbed—tail.

Kinds of Cats

There are many kinds of **breeds** or types of cat. Different breeds have different characteristics. For example, some breeds are long-haired, some are short-haired, and some grow to be large, while others stay small. Some cat breeds have long tails, while others have bobbed or short tails. A **pure-bred** cat (sometimes called a pedigree cat) is a cat that had parents and grandparents that belong to the same breed. A purebred will usually have the characteristics of the breed. A **mixed-breed cat** has parents that belong to different breeds. A mixed breed may display a mixture of characteristics from a variety of breeds. Whether you decide on a purebred cat or a mixed breed, learning about the characteristics of different breeds can help you choose a feline friend. One of the main ways to examine some of the different breeds is by comparing their **coats** or fur. The following breeds are some of the popular long-haired and short-haired breeds.

Long-Haired Breeds

PERSIAN

A Persian cat has a large head, tiny ears, a short nose, and big round eyes. Its coat of long, silky hair is beautiful, but needs to be brushed very often. These cats come in many colors. Some are pure white, red, or black. Others are a mix of black and white. Many Persians have stripes or coats with three different colors.

Fluffy Persians can come in a variety of colors.

Compared to some other breeds, Persians tend to be larger. An adult male can weigh up to ten pounds. Persians are also known for their gentle nature. Most are quiet, calm, and enjoy sitting quietly while you pet and cuddle them.

HIMALAYAN

This breed of cat looks a lot like a Persian cat. A Himalayan has a big head and big round eyes like a Persian. Sometimes, a Himalayan's eyes are blue. The Himalayan also has long, thick hair that requires a lot of grooming. A Himalayan's coat is usually a light color, like white, soft gold, or tan. Some Himalayans can also be chocolate colored.

The Himalayan has short legs and is not as big as the Persian. If you want a long-haired cat that is more active than a Persian, the Himalayan might be a good choice. These cats can be quiet, but they also like to play.

Short-Haired Breeds

AMERICAN SHORTHAIR

Known for its sweet nature, the American shorthair makes a good family pet. This cat has a very strong, medium-sized body, but it is very gentle. The coat of the American shorthair is thick but does not need a lot of brushing. Petting this cat actually keeps its coat shiny. The American shorthair comes in many different colors. These

This shorthaired calico cat uses its claws on a tree trunk. Calico cats have coats with patches of different colors.

THE MAINE COON

Neither a long-haired nor a short-haired breed, the Maine Coon is one of the oldest cat breeds in North America. It was probably first bred in Maine, and is actually Maine's official state cat. The Maine Coon probably got its name from the fact that it has a bushy tail and coloring that sometimes resembles a raccoon's. A Maine Coon cat's coat is thick, but not as long as a Persian's or Himalayan's. The fur can come in a wide range of colors, from white to black, striped or spotted.

These cats are pretty large, with adults weighing anywhere from ten to eighteen pounds. Maine Coons are known for their playfulness, which is why some people think they are one of the best breeds.

cats may have coats of one, two, or three colors. The colors can show up as stripes, spots, or patches. Most American shorthairs get along well with other cats and dogs.

MANX

The Manx looks like many other cats except for one thing—it does not have a tail. People who own this breed do not seem to care that it has no tail.

They say this type of cat is very smart and very playful, which makes a Manx a good pet. But Manx cats are rare, which means they might be hard to find. The number of Manx kittens born each year is far less than other breeds.

Though some Manx cats have short stubs instead of tails, most Manx cats are completely tailless.

Abyssinians can have tawny—or light brown—coats and golden eyes.

ABYSSINIAN

Some people believe the Abyssinians look like the sacred cats of ancient Egypt. The Abyssinian has large pointed ears and eyes shaped like almonds. An Abyssinian has a long tail and slim, long legs. Its coat is soft and silky, and can come in many solid colors. Like most shorthairs, the Abyssinian does not need a lot of brushing.

SPHYNX

The Sphynx looks like it has no hair. However, people who own this breed say this cat is not completely hairless. The Sphynx probably has the shortest hair of all other cat breeds, and obviously, does not need to be brushed. Like most breeds, the Sphynx likes attention, is very curious, and will often get into trouble. If you decide on this breed, you will find that your cat likes to cuddle up with you, especially on cold nights.

People with Sphynx cats say that the fine hair on the cats' bodies reminds them of the fuzz on the outside of a peach. Because it does not have thick fur to protect its skin, a Sphynx needs special care to keep its skin healthy.

The first Siamese cats originated in Southeast Asia.

SIAMESE

At first glance, you may think a Siamese cat looks a bit unusual. Its ears may look too big for its thin face. Siamese cats have narrow eyes, small mouths, and long and skinny tails to match their long and skinny bodies. Most of the Siamese's coat is tan or white. The darker coloring is in the cat's tail, feet, ears, and face. Many cat owners say that Siamese are noisier than a lot of other breeds. Siamese like to "talk," which means they meow a lot. They also have a lot of energy.

Cat breeders often have many kittens or young cats to choose from.

Where to Find a Cat

Once you have decided that you want a cat, you will then have to figure out where to get your cat. If you want a purebred cat, you should look for a cat **breeder.** A breeder is a person who raises certain breeds of cats. Many breeders have kittens or adult cats for sale. Most cat breeders have advertisements in local newspapers or online. You can also ask a local vet for any cat breeders he or she may recommend.

Some breeders raise their cats to participate in cat shows. At these shows, cats are judged based on their physical traits and how they compare to what the breed should look like. If you are still thinking about what kind of cat to get, attending a local cat show is a good way to see many different types of cats. Most breeders who attend or participate in shows are happy to tell you about their cats. Some of them might even have kittens ready for new homes.

You can also adopt a cat—and sometimes kittens—from breed rescue organizations. These groups specialize in finding good homes for specific breeds. For example, there may be several Persian rescue organizations in different states across the country. The cats that have been rescued are strays or were given up because their owners could no longer take care of them. If

Cats and kittens in shelters and humane societies are just waiting to be adopted into loving homes.

29

you are interested in adopting one of their cats, breed rescuers will ask you many questions to make sure you can offer a cat a good home. They will also tell you where the cat came from and if the cat has any problems or special needs. You can find breed rescue groups on the Internet.

Animal shelters—which may be called humane societies or animal welfare societies—always have a large number of cats and kittens looking for good homes. Most of the cats at shelters are mixed breeds, but you may also find several purebreds. Like the cats in breed rescue groups, the cats at shelters have been abandoned or given up by their owners. Some of the kittens at shelters were found in backyards or in the woods.

Healthy kittens are playful and aware of what is going on around them.

Whether you get your cat from a breeder, rescue organization, or shelter, always look carefully at the cats and their surroundings. Do the cats and kittens look healthy? Does it look like the breeders, rescue groups, or shelters provide enough space, food, and water for the cats? Is the cats' living area clean? If the answer to any of these questions is "no" then you should not get your cat from that place. It is likely that the cats have been mistreated and are unhealthy. Besides checking out the cats and where they are kept, you should also feel free to ask a few questions. Asking the right questions will help you to bring home a happy and healthy pet that is perfect for you. Some of these questions include

- How long has the breeder/rescue group/shelter been raising and adopting out or selling cats?
- If the cat is at a shelter or from a rescue group, why is it there?
- How long has it been there?
- Has the cat had all the basic **shots** it needs?
- Does the cat have special medical needs?
- Is the cat mainly an indoor or outdoor cat?
- Does the cat get along with children? (Some cats prefer adults.)
- Does the cat get along with other animals, such as dogs or another cat?

Also, do not forget to play with the cat or kitten to see how it reacts to being petted and held. Making sure you like each other is an important before step before bringing home your new friend.

4

Life with Your Cat

Before you bring your new friend home, you must prepare for its arrival. One of the first steps is to find a local vet and schedule an appointment for your cat. Try to take your cat to the vet soon after you bring it home. The vet will check your cat to make sure that he or she looks okay. The vet may also give the cat some shots or medicine that it needs to stay healthy. This first vet appointment is also a good time to ask any questions you may have about caring for your cat. Vets are happy to give advice that will help your cat settle into its new home.

There are several basic things that you must get before you bring your cat home. All of these things can be found at your local pet store or supermarket.

This cat loves being cuddled by his best friend.

Collars and Tags

Whether your cat is an indoor cat or an outdoor cat, it should always wear a collar around its neck. The collar is used to hang important tags. These tags—which can be metal or plastic—have important information. The tags may say whether or not your cat has received certain shots that are required by law. (The vet will give you these tags when your cat gets the shot.) Tags may also have information, such as your cat's name, your home address, and your phone number. If your cat gets lost or runs away, an identification (or ID) tag can help people bring your cat back to you. Sometimes this information is printed or sewn onto the collar itself.

Some owners do not use collars for their cats. This is because they are afraid that the collar will get hooked on things as the cat runs and climbs around. If the collar gets stuck on something, the cat could choke or get hurt while trying to free itself. One solution is to use special breakaway collars. These collars—found in pet stores—break apart when they get stuck on something. But even with breakaway collars, some cat owners do

Most veterinarians offer a service that further protects your cat if it gets loose. Vets can put a small microchip just beneath your cat's skin. This chip holds the same information that an ID tag would have. If your cat gets lost, a shelter or vet's office can scan the chip and find out who the cat belongs to. Many vets recommend these chips in addition to collars and tags because tags and collars can break or fall off.

not want to risk having their cat get hurt. You should discuss all collar options with your vet when you bring your cat in to be examined.

Food and Water

Your cat will need its own food and water dishes. These dishes can be small or large—depending upon the size of your cat—and can be made of metal or plastic. Pet stores have a large variety of dishes to choose from.

Two short-haired brothers share a meal.

DANGER!

There are many foods, chemicals, plants, and household items that are dangerous to your cat. If your cat eats or gets into any of the following things, call your veterinarian or animal hospital.

FOODS
- chocolate
- coffee or tea
- onions
- grapes and raisins
- fish or chicken bones
- human medication or vitamin supplements
- nuts
- mushrooms

HOUSEHOLD ITEMS
- cleaning products like soap or bleach
- antifreeze (for cars)
- rubber bands
- string
- coins
- human toys—metal, plastic, small, or large
- glue
- moth balls
- pesticides used to kill bugs or rodents

PLANTS
- aloe vera
- azalea
- baby's breath
- lilies
- holly
- irises
- daffodils
- foxglove

Your cat should always have clean water available for drinking. You should check its water dish often to make sure that it stays clean. Your cat may also tip over the dish and spill its water when it is running around or playing.

Cats need to be fed every day—for some, many times a day. Pet stores, grocery stores, and vet offices sell food that has been specially made for a cat. There is dry food that comes in a bag or a box, and wet food that is kept in pouches or cans. Talk to your vet about what kind of diet would be good for your cat. Cats can eat some human food, but you should be very careful what you feed it. Some human food can make your cat fat, sick, or can even poison it.

Litter Boxes

Indoor cats and kittens can be trained to go to the bathroom in a specific place. This spot is usually a litter box. Most litter boxes are made of plastic and are deep enough to hold some form of cat (or kitty) litter. Litter can be bought at pet stores or grocery stores. The litter may be in powder form, or it may be small clumps or pieces. Some kitty litter is specially

Pet stores sell handheld scoopers that can help you keep your cat's litter box clean.

scented to hide odors, while others are made from recycled material. The litter absorbs the cat's waste, making it easier for you to clean up after it.

Cats are very intelligent and most do not require a lot of training to use the litter box. Many cat owners suggest showing your cat the litter box (so it knows where it is) and praising the cat whenever it uses it properly. After the first few times it uses the litter box, a cat usually knows that it should always go to the bathroom there.

You must always keep your cat's litter box clean. Most cat owners suggest scooping out the wet or dirty parts every night, while leaving the dry litter inside the litter box. Every four days you should completely change the litter and wash out the litter box. This will help keep your home clean and can also protect you and your cat from getting sick.

Grooming

You do not have to bathe your cat very often. Cats are naturally clean animals. Most cats groom themselves several times a day. You may see your cat

Many cats love being brushed since it feels like they are being petted. Cats with longer hair must be brushed often.

licking its paws and then wiping its face or other parts of its body. If you do have to wash your cat, make sure you use shampoo or soap that is made especially for cats.

If your cat has medium or long hair, you need to brush it often. Long-haired cats that are not groomed properly will develop tangles or knots in their coats. This can be very painful for the cats and makes it harder for you to keep them clean. Pet stores sell different types of combs and brushes you can use on your cat.

Other Supplies

Like most pets, cats like to sleep a lot. Some cats will rest in quiet corners. Others like to stretch out on the floor or on a window ledge. Many cats like to sleep on couches, beds, or baskets that you use. Some small kittens will even curl up to rest in your shoes! You should make a bed for your cat so that it has a place of its own. Pet stores sell soft or fuzzy cat beds. You can also make your own using a sturdy basket or small box and a soft pillow or blankets.

This kitten loves to nap on its bed. When it is awake, it can watch the world outside the window.

Many cats will snuggle into any comfortable spot—between couch cushions, pillows, in laundry baskets, or even in the sleeves of your shirts.

Cats have sharp claws and they like to use them. In the wild, they keep their claws short by running around on rough ground or scratching at hard things like trees. It is natural for your cat to want to scratch things in your home. You can keep your cat from scratching up your curtains and furniture by buying a scratching post. These posts come in a variety of shapes, sizes, and colors. It gives the cat a safe place for it to use its claws. Your cat's claws will also need to be trimmed every so often. Ask your vet about how to do this.

Cats love to play. You should provide your cat with toys that will keep it entertained and happy. Most cats love things that roll around or dangle from a string. Some people make homemade toys for their cats to play with. However, the safest thing to do is to buy toys that are specially made to withstand your

You can buy scratching posts in a variety of shapes or sizes. Toys attached to the post can keep your cat entertained for hours.

41

BODY LANGUAGE

Cats communicate with each other and with humans through body movements and sounds. Many cat owners believe that cats can "talk" with their tails. Usually, when a cat's tail hangs low, it feels very safe and calm. However, unlike a dog, when a cat wags its tail slowly, it might be ready to pounce on a mouse or toy or it might be telling you to back away and leave it alone. Each cat is different, so take some time to learn your cat's body language.

These kittens love to watch objects move across the television screen. You must always make sure that furniture, electronics, or other heavy objects will not fall on your cat.

When a cat rubs its head or body against you, it wants attention and affection.

cat's claws and teeth. Make sure the toys cannot break easily and do not have small pieces that your cat can swallow or choke upon.

Some toys have catnip in them. Catnip is a plant that cats love to smell. In the wild, cats would rub up against and

This cat is happy to snuggle up while her friend does homework.

scratch at catnip plants. Catnip toys can provide hours of fun for your cat.

There are many more things that you can learn about cats, but the best teacher you will find is your cat. Spend a lot of time with your cat, and you will begin to understand it better. Cats do not have words to use, but they will still let you know what they want. By listening to its meows or watching the way it moves its feet, tail, or ears, you can start to understand your cat. Is it asking for food? Does it want to play? Does it want you to pick it up for a cuddle?

With care, time, patience, and a lot of love, you and your feline friend can have many happy years of fun.

Glossary

allergies—The body's reaction to something that bothers it. People can be allergic to plants, food, and animals like cats.

breed—A specific type of animal that has certain characteristics or traits.

breeder—A person who raises specific types of cats. Cats and kittens from a breeder may participate in cat shows or are sold to good homes.

coat—The fur of the cat. Cat coats can be long, short, and may come in many different colors and textures.

litter box—A place where indoor cats go to the bathroom. These boxes are filled with litter that absorbs the cat's waste.

mixed-breed cat—A cat that belongs to more than one breed of cat.

purebred—A cat with parents and grandparents that belonged to one specific breed.

shots—Special medicine that a vet injects into your pet using a needle. Shots can prevent and treat many illnesses.

stray—An animal that has no home. Many stray pets are taken to shelters to find new homes.

veterinarian—A doctor who treats animals. A veterinarian is called a vet for short.

Find Out More

Books

Barnes, Julia. *Pet Cats*. Milwaukee, WI: Gareth Stevens, 2007.

Jones, Annie. *All about Cats*. New York: Chelsea House, 2005.

Ring, Susan. *Caring for Your Cat*. Mankato, MN: Weigl Publishers, 2003.

Silverstein, Alvin & Virginia. *Curious Cats*. Brookfield, CT: Twenty-First Century Books, 2003.

Simon, Seymour. *Cats*. New York: HarperCollins Publishers, 2004.

Web Sites

Cat Care from ASPCA's ANIMALAND

http://www.aspca.org/site/PageServer?pagename=kids_pc_cat_411

The American Society for the Prevention of Cruelty to Animals (ASPCA) sponsors this site for kids who want to learn more about caring for a pet cat. The Web site features games, activity sheets, cartoons, and a lot of information about caring for many different types of pets.

Cat Fancier's Web Site

http://www.fanciers.com

This Web site is updated by cat breeders, exhibitors, show judges, veterinarians, and other cat lovers from around the world. The site offers tips on caring for your cat, descriptions of different cat breeds, and more.

Cats! Wild to Mild!

http://www.nhm.org/cats

This site is sponsored by the Natural History Museum of Los Angeles County. It has information about cat mythology, behavior, responsible pet care, and more.

PAWS Kids Creating a Kinder World for Animals
http://www.pawskids.org/pets/pet_care/cats.html
On this Web site you can find fun facts about cats and a lot of tips for keeping a healthy cat.

Purebred Cat Rescue
http://purebredcatbreedrescue.org/rescues.htm
This Web site will direct you to breed rescue organizations all over the United States.

About the Author

Joyce Hart is a freelance writer who lives outside of Seattle, Washington. She has owned several different mixed-breed cats and kittens. One of her favorite kittens used to sit on the kitchen table and wait for the family's big dog to walk by. The kitten would then jump on the dog's back, hold on tight, and enjoy the short ride.

Index

Page numbers for illustrations are in **bold**.